MY WORLD

Donna Bryant

Illustrated by Rebecca Archer

HODDER AND STOUGHTON
LONDON SYDNEY AUCKLAND

My Name

Everyone has a name.
What is your name?
Are you named after
someone in your family?

Billy

from Kim

Zena

My name is

Some names have a special meaning.

Felix: happy
Sarah: princess
Erin: peace
Leo: lion

Frances: free
Ezra: helper
Lulu: rabbit
Charles: strong

Does your name have a meaning?

A nickname is for fun. It's not your real name.
People have all sorts of funny nicknames.

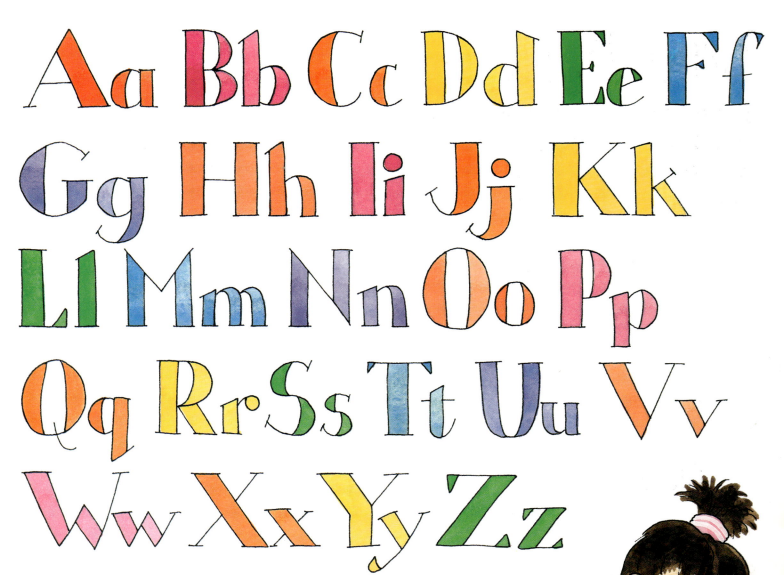

Aa Bb Cc Dd Ee Ff
Gg Hh Ii Jj Kk
Ll Mm Nn Oo Pp
Qq Rr Ss Tt Uu Vv
Ww Xx Yy Zz

Each letter in your name is in the alphabet.
Point to the letters in your name.
You could copy them on to paper or card.

Ask your mum or dad why they gave you your special name.

My Family

When you were born, you became part of a family.
Families are all different sizes.
How many people are there in your family?
Some families live together in the same house
and some live in different houses.

Which members of your family live with you?

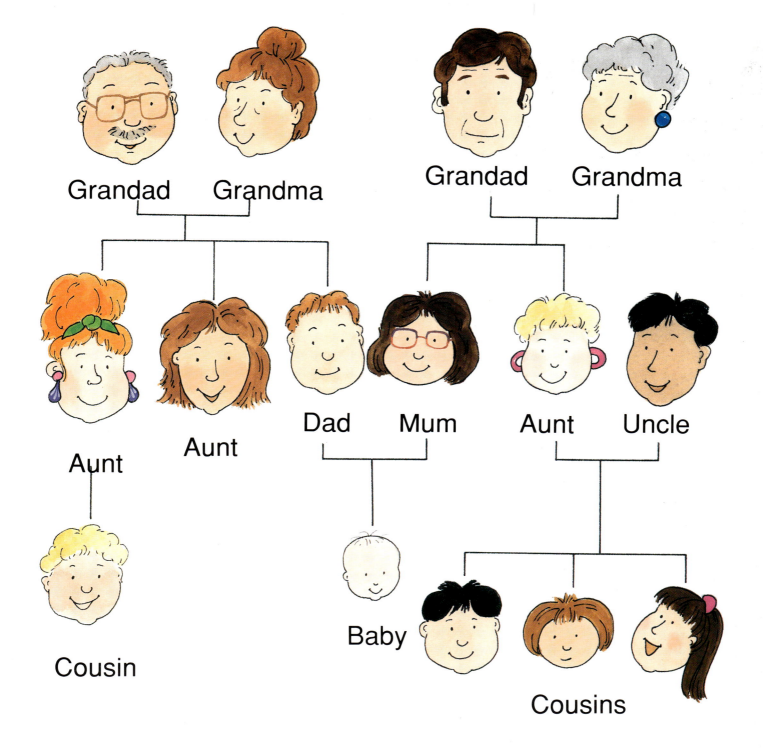

Grandad   Grandma   Grandad   Grandma

Aunt   Aunt   Dad   Mum   Aunt   Uncle

Cousin   Baby

Cousins

Draw a picture of your family on a big sheet of paper.
Draw a line between the parents and children. This
is your family tree.

My Body

People come in all shapes and sizes. We come in many colours. Our eyes and hair are different colours too. What colour are your eyes? Do you have straight hair or curly hair?

You are special. Nobody else is exactly the same as you. Some people look alike but they are not the same. You have your own name, your own voice, your own thoughts. You have your own body.

Growth Chart

Lie down on a big piece of paper.
Ask someone to draw around you.
Colour in the big picture of yourself.
Can you name the parts of your body?

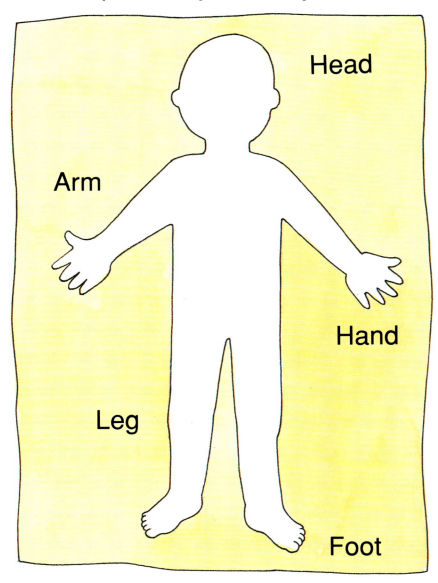

Pin the picture to the wall. You can stand in front
of it and see how much you have grown.

How My Body Works

All the parts of your body work together so that you grow, move and stay healthy.

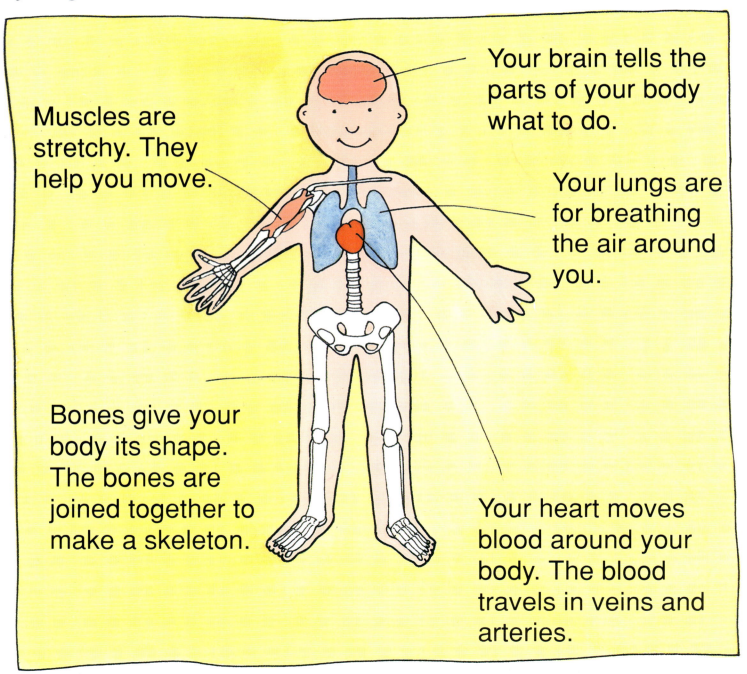

Your brain tells the parts of your body what to do.

Muscles are stretchy. They help you move.

Your lungs are for breathing the air around you.

Bones give your body its shape. The bones are joined together to make a skeleton.

Your heart moves blood around your body. The blood travels in veins and arteries.

Senses

When you hear, see, smell, taste and touch,
you are using your senses.

I hear with my . . .

I see with my . . .

I smell with my . . .

I taste with my . . .

I touch with my . . .   Your brain will tell you the answers!

All sorts of wonderful things are going on inside your
body. Your body even grows new skin if you fall over
and graze yourself.

Food

To grow and stay healthy you need food and drink.
We all like and eat different foods.
What do you like to eat?

Some food looks very
different when it is cooked.

People eat in different ways.

Tasty!

Put small pieces of food on a plate. Close your eyes or wear a blindfold. Taste each piece of food. Try to guess what you are eating.

Don't forget to clean your teeth afterwards

You have teeth so you can bite and chew your food. Dentists help you look after your teeth.

Keeping Healthy

Exercise is fun, especially if you are out in the fresh air. The oxygen in the air gives you energy. You also need many different foods to give you energy and keep you healthy.

Wash your hands before you eat, and after you have been to the toilet.

When I have my hair washed, I pretend it's raining!

Washing your body in the bath or shower makes your body clean. You feel good too.

Your body needs rest. That's why you go to bed. After a good sleep, you'll be ready to play again.

When I Am Ill

If you feel very sick or have a pain, the doctor will help you to feel well again. The doctor may look at your tongue and throat and check your ears and eyes.

ALWAYS WEAR A HAT IN THE SUN!

A Doctor's Kit
Scraps of material for bandages

Lolly stick as splint

Yoghurt pot and string stethoscope

Do you know how to phone for help in an emergency? Ask your mum or dad to show you.

If you have to go to hospital, you will have
your own bed. You can take your favourite toys
with you. Your family and friends will visit you.

Soon you will go home again.

An optician makes glasses to
help people see more clearly.

A hearing aid helps some
people to hear sounds.

My Clothes

People wear all sorts of clothes.
Do you have clothes for playing and different
clothes for special days?
Some people wear a uniform to school. Do you?

Hats

A hat protects you from the sun, the rain or the cold. You can wear a hat just for fun. Here are some ideas:

Shoes

Shoes protect your feet.
Can you sort these shoes into pairs?

My Home

Where you live is called your home.
Your home is a shelter for you and your family.
It keeps you warm and dry.

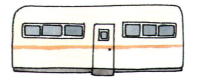

Homes are made from many different things.
All homes have walls, a ceiling and a floor.
What is your home made from?
Does it look like any of these?

Inside

How many rooms are there at your place?
You could draw a picture of each room.
What is in each room? Where do you sleep?
Do you know your address?

Which rooms do these belong in?

Playing

Everyone loves to play.
You can play on your own or with your friends.
What is going on in this picture?

How many red things can you see?
How many blue things?

What do you like playing best of all?

My Friends

Friends can be big or small.
Friends are the people and things you like.
Friends do things together. Friends play,
share things and sometimes fight.

Friends keep you company
and comfort you.

Friends know how
you are feeling
because they care
about you.

Some friends live with you and some live a long way away.

Friends are everywhere!
Friends talk

sing

dance

make things

paint

play together.

Friends are fun.

Friends sit together

share secrets and books

play games

tell stories.

Friends look after one another.

What do you like doing with your friends?

In the Street

There are all sorts of shops in the street.
Where do you go to post a letter?
What do you do at the library?

Where would you buy these things?

Playing shops

You can set up a shop at home. Use buttons and paper as money. You can sell all sorts of things in your shop. Take turns to be assistant.

Take Care Out There!
The road is for traffic. Remember the road is a dangerous place.
1. Hold a grown-up's hand when you are near a road.
2. NEVER run out on to the road.
3. Don't play near a road.

IF SOMEONE YOU DON'T KNOW ASKS YOU TO GET IN THEIR CAR, SAY 'NO'. TELL YOUR MUM OR DAD OR A TEACHER ABOUT IT.

On the Move

People and things travel from one place to another in all sorts of vehicles.
How do you like to travel?

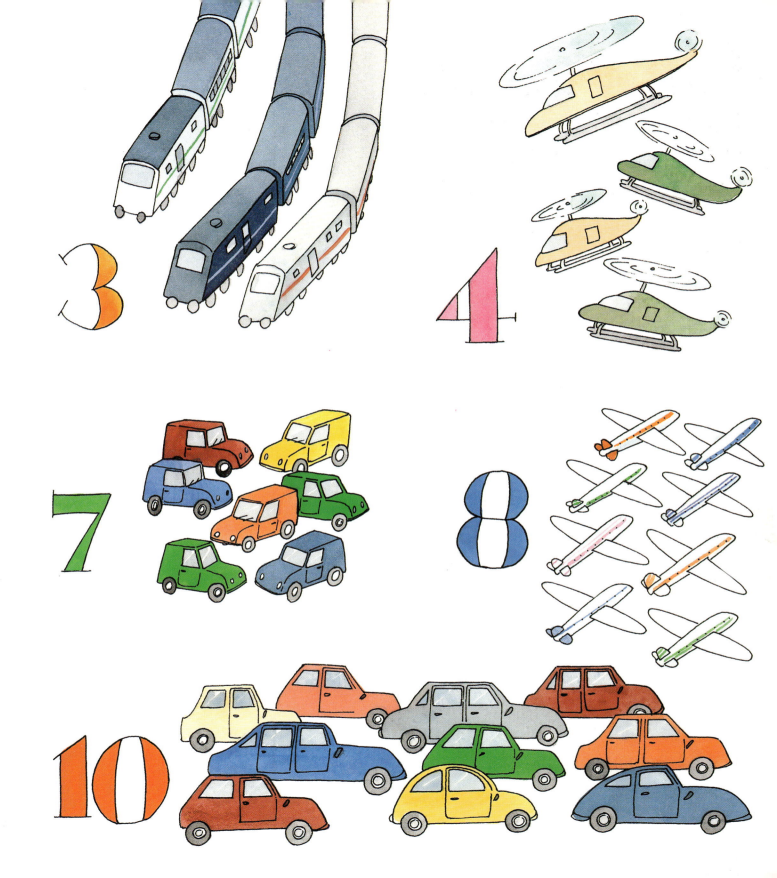

Weather

What is the weather like today? Look at the sky.
What colour is it? Are there any clouds?

It's raining!

Rain is water that falls from the clouds. Everything needs water.

It's sunny!

The sun keeps us warm. On sunny days it is fun to play outside.

It's windy!

You can't see the wind but you can see the things it blows.

It's snowing!

When the weather is very cold, snow falls.

When the sun shines through the rain,
you may see a rainbow.
Red
Orange
Yellow
Green
Blue
Indigo
Violet

Which of these things go together?

Growing Things

All living things need water. Grow a bean, a carrot top or a bulb in water.

Seeds
From a tiny seed a plant grows. Plant seeds in the garden or a window box.
Don't forget to water them.

A sunflower seed can grow into a flower that is taller than you are.

Baby animals

As baby animals grow up they learn to do new things ...
just as you do.
Do you know the names of these animals? Can you
match each baby with its mother?

Be gentle with all living things.

My Books

Books are special. They are found all over the world.

Make a book of your paintings, or from blank paper and then write in it . Use the point of a pencil to make two holes in each page. Join the pages together with wool or string.

Goodnight!

Everyone loves a book at bedtime.